I0503622

Guide to profitable Returns in Real Estate Investment

Contents

Copyright © Prince Abraham 2019

All rights reserved. No part of this publication may be reproduced, stored in a retrieval system, or transmitted in any form by any means electronic, mechanical, photocopying, recording or otherwise, without the prior written permission of the author.

ISBN: 9781709560064

INTRODUCTION

According to Savills world research, *"The value of global property in 2015 amounted to 2.7 times the world's GDP, making up roughly 60% of mainstream global assets and representing an important store of national, corporate and individual wealth. Residential property accounted for 75% of the total value of global property."*

Having this in mind, it is worth saying that real estate is a gold mine with lots of opportunities, and potentials for wealth creation and is worth the interest of any investor, individual or business person who wishes to tap from the massive potentials of real estate by investing in it.

However, it is very important that such a person should first have a basic understanding of what real estate is all about. *Guide to profitable Returns in Real Estate Investment*, has been written to help you make informed decisions about how to invest and make significant income from real estate investment.

This guide covers the fundamentals of real estate investment such as what is real estate, categories of real estate, cash flow analysis, tips on how to finance your first property as a beginner, best way to make money through real estate, etc.

As you go through this guide, you would be informed on the basics you need to know to get started, and you'd be more than prepared to hit the ground running with your very first real estate investment.

WHAT IS REAL ESTATE

The word real estate can be comprehensively defined as the Land, air rights above and below the land, property and anything fixed, immovable, or permanently attached to it, which can be bought, leased, sold, or transferred together or separately.

The term real estate refers to real, or physical property. The word "Real" comes from the Latin root *res*, or things. Some would say it's from the Latin word *rex,* which means "royal," since kings used to own all land in their kingdoms.

REAL ESTATE INVESTMENT

A real estate investment is the purchase of a property with the primary goal of earning income or returns from the said property through rental or resale but not as a primary residence and thus increasing your financial statement in the long term.

Any property bought, leased, together or separately without any intentions of making profits either in the short term or long term cannot be classified as a real estate investment.

CATEGORIES OF REAL ESTATE

There are different types of real estate. Each of these have their unique opportunities, utilities and purposes. Below are descriptions of the four major categories of real estate.

LAND REAL ESTATE

The basic commodity for all types of real property/ real estate investment is the land. Developers would procure the land, merge it with different properties, which is also known as assembly and assign it so they can increase the value of the property. Any person or group of persons (real estate agents) specialized in the sale of large tracks of undeveloped land is known as a land broker.

CATEGORIES OF LAND REAL ESTATE

a. **Undeveloped Land**: An undeveloped land is any area that lacks any form of infrastructure, buildings or services. They are also known as urban developments.

b. **Land in Transition or Early Development**: These are lands set aside for specific purposes or use. This means that their use or intended use has already been decided.

c. **Site Location/Assembling Parcels**: This is the purchase or acquisition of land from various owners by a broker for a specific use. This often requires negotiations in order to acquire enough adjacent lands from neighbors for a proposed development or project.

d. **Subdivision and Lot Selling**: Here, developers would purchase an undeveloped land, get necessary approvals, subdivide it and install utilities or other infrastructure. After these, they let land brokers wholesale the lots to builders for either residential or other infrastructure construction/development.

e. **Farms and Ranches**: These are lands used for large scale farming or ranching. They

BENEFITS OF LAND REAL ESTATE.

Land real estate offers a number of opportunities that many investors fail to see. These opportunities can make a good investment for the many who recognize that they exist and invest in them.

Quite a number of number of investors overlook the opportunities of vacant/undeveloped lands as a result of value misconceptions and erroneous assumptions about land investments. Below we shall explore some common misconceptions of land investment and outline the benefits of investing in land real estate.

1. Land Is A Tangible Asset

By "tangible asset" we mean that land is material and has physical existence. This means it can be seen, touched, felt and can be used by choice. This produces a sense of ownership and comfort knowing that one is investing in something that exist physically.

2. Affordability

Depending on your investment preference and capacity, land real estate provides one of the most affordable investment opportunities. It is quiet affordable buying vacant lands than buying lands with structures on it. High property prices can become a real financial struggle and challenge especially in the major cities.

Land real estate also offers you the opportunity to begin your real estate investment with less capital and also offers you an array of options on what to do with the land. You can decide to build on it, rent/lease or let it appreciate before resell. Also, property tax and insurance rates are much lower when buying vacant land. Land investment does not also require you to hire or pay property managers to supervise the vacant land, or manage tenants.

3. Little To No Maintenance

Vacant lands are very easily maintained over time as compared to residential, commercial or farms. There are no needs for renovations or anything like it, besides mowing lawns to keep the land neat and tidy pending usage or sale. Undeveloped lands are long term, hands off investments which takes little effort or time.

4. Long-Term Appreciation

Being a tangible investment, land real estate (undeveloped land) will almost always remain in the same condition over a long period of time. Except for cases of natural disaster such as floods and fire which may affect the value of land in the short term, the land eventually recovers from such occurrences over time and appreciates in value. The value of land has always been known to appreciate in value though the rate of value appreciation would depend on some other factors.

This appreciation in value is typically dependent on the economic growth and activity within the area the land is located. For instance, an area where development has started to thrive, or is undergoing rezoning in other to become a commercial or industrial center, would witness a surge in the values of lands within the area..

5. Less Competition

Real estate investing is usually highly competitive in areas of high value and ROI. However, undeveloped land is often undervalued and less competitive. This is so because real estate investors would often overlook smaller amount of competition in land investing, opting for commercial, residential or industrial properties.

Investing in land real estate would often give better returns on investment as there are much less competition to deal with.

THINGS TO NOTE BEFORE INVESTING IN LAND REAL ESTATE

While investing in land real estate is less competitive and guarantees a good return on investment (ROI), it is necessary to put certain considerations in check before investing in land real estate. Below are two import things to consider

1. What Can Be Developed on The Land?

The uses of land are numerous if not endless. However, it is important to understand that zoning requirements can restrict what can be built on a particular land within a location.

Zoning is the restriction on the way land within a jurisdiction can be used. Zoning laws enable governmental agencies ensure that communities are safe, functional and property values are preserved. Zoning places restrictions on certain activities within a location. For instance, through zoning, a gun store would not be allowed to be cited next to a school; an adult club would also not be allowed to operate next to a playground.

Notwithstanding, anything can be developed on vacant land, this includes but not limited to the following:

- Strip mall
- Hospital
- Single-family home
- Multi-family home
- Office space
- Hotel
- Resort
- Mall
- Farm
- Parking lot
- Retail space
- Mixed retail and residential space

2. What Is Your Goal in Purchasing Land?

Before proceeding to invest in land real estate, it is also important to decide before hand your objectives or interest for the investment. Your goal or interest would go a long way in determining the strategy to consider for the investment. There are different investment strategies to consider and we shall outline them briefly. As a rule, these strategies are not a one size fits all approach as two different investors could have varying approaches for same land. The overall outlook here is to determine the strategy that will yield the best ROI for the investment.

a. **Buy And Sell (Flipping)**:
The buy and sell land investment strategy basically involves flipping of the land (we shall discuss flipping in details in a subsequent section). Here you acquire a land believed to be below the market value and hope to find a buyer who will buy at market value or more. In buy and sell, you hope for a quick sale making little or no additional changes to the land.

b. **Buy and hold**:
In this strategy, the investor acquires a land and holds on to it for a period of time pending an increase in value of the land. In buy and hold, you will have pay taxes and bear any additional costs in maintaining the

land prior to sale. This strategy is commonly used in areas that are being rezoned or opening up to economic growth and development.

c. **Buy, develop, and hold**:

In this strategy, the goal of purchasing is to develop it yourself. The structures could be anything of your choice such as a complex of townhouses which will be rented out to residential tenants, a strip mall for retail tenants, etc. over the years, the value of the land equally appreciates in value.

d. **Buy, cultivate, and hold**:

This strategy is best suited for ranches or farms. Here, the interest is more on the actual land than on the structures to be built. It could be used for cultivating crops, livestock rearing or any other purpose aimed more at utilizing the land. In buy, cultivate and hold, the soil type, location, weather conditions are often major factors for consideration before purchase, as these affects the use of the land.

e. **Buy, go through entitlement process, and sell**:

In this category, the land is purchased and taken through the legal process of having the land zoned for a specific use. For instance, if there are lots of land zoned for commercial use within the location and the area is now developed and would make a good site for high-rise residential building, you could get it rezoned for residential use. By doing this, the value of the land would appreciate as it will be more desirable for potential developers who would not want to go through the process of rezoning it themselves.

f. **Buy, develop, and sell**:

In buy, develop and sell, the interest is to develop the land yourself maybe for residential, commercial or industrial and sell directly to an end user. For instance, you buy a land, develop it by build a twain duplex and sell directly to a company looking to acquire a residential house for their top management staff.

g. **Buy, develop, and rent**:

Finally, you could decide to buy, develop the land and rent the land to either an end user or an agency to manage for you.

The above mentioned strategies outline different goals of investing in land real estate. As has been stated already, each of this strategies can be adopted depending on what the end goal is. It is therefore very necessary to understand and choose appropriately to avoid loss of investment.

RISK FACTORS TO CONSIDER IN LAND INVESTMENT

An undeveloped land has so many possibilities and potentials for good returns on investment. However, we shall look at some risk factors to consider when investing in land real estate as there are no investments without risks. Understanding these risk factors and applying great caution in avoiding or mitigating them will ultimately yield good ROI. These risk factors include;

1. Zoning Classification

The first risk factor to consider when investing in land real estate is the zoning classifications the land maybe subjected to. The zoning classification stipulates how the land can be used which might not be suitable to you or potential buyers and thus will affect the potential value of the land. Every town has a zoning classification which divides the town into varying category for use such as industrial, commercial, residential, historical etc.

If for example the land is zoned for commercial use and you intend using it for residential, then there might be a challenge. However, if you want to change the zoning of a land, you will need to follow a process of reclassification as some classifications are very old and would be reclassified if the intended use or new classification fits the current status of the town. Other times, reclassification might not be very easy to achieve.

2. Zoning Restrictions

The second risk factor to look out for when investing in land real estate is how much size for development is permitted. These include:

I. **Lot coverage**: The lot coverage is put in place to prevent flooding issues. It is a code that stipulates the percentage of land which mustn't be covered for access to rain/drainage to avoiding flooding other neighboring properties.

II. **Height**: knowing the allowable height for any structure within the location of the land is also important as this determines the height your structure is restricted to. If for instance your investment goal is to erect a four-story residential building which will yield a better returns, but the town has a restriction of not more than two stories, then your investment yield will be greatly affected as you can't build more than the allowable height.

III. **Setback requirements:** The setback requirements are codes which stipulates the required distance your property is to maintain from the neighboring property lines. This would include the front and back lines, and the two sides. Depending on the lot size of the land, this could also affect the size of any structure that can be built.

IV. **Floor area ratio:** In some towns, the total floor area is limited to a certain percentage of the lot size. The square footage is added together and divided by the lot size.

V. **Accessory buildings:** There are also code restrictions for structures such as sheds and garages. These codes might also restrict the number of parking spaces a property should have.

3. Access to Utilities.

Investment in land real estate should take into careful consideration the ease of access to utilities. These utilities includes electricity, telephone, running water, cable, sewer, internet, etc.

If these basic utilities are lacking or are nowhere close to the land, this could spell disaster for any potential development, as these utilities are very expensive to install which ultimately will affect your investment and potential profit.

4. Environmental Factors

Another risk factor to be considered in land real estate investment are the environmental factors of the property. These includes the soil suitability for certain kinds of buildings or purposes, the location of the land which might be prone to certain environmental issues, etc. These are necessary to be considered before investing in land real estate.

5. No Income, but Expenses

In land real estate, income is not quickly generated except on a quick land flipping circumstance. Also it is quite difficult to obtain loan on an undeveloped land which means purchase might have to be cash, thereby tying up funds for other investment. Also undeveloped land would only incur expenses such as taxes and maintenance costs pending next action on the land.

RESIDENTIAL REAL ESTATE

The residential real estate is the most common type of real estate that most people are familiar with. The residential real estate comprises of both new constructions and resale homes. They include; single-family homes, condominiums, apartments, townhouses, quad lexes, triple-deckers, duplexes and many other types of living arrangements.

CATEGORIES OF RESIDENTIAL REAL ESTATE

When investing in residential real estate, it is very imperative to know the different categories of residential homes available and which category would suit your investment interest or goal.

We shall briefly examine the pros and cons of some more common categories of the residential real estate.

1. Multi-Family Home

The multi-family residential houses are houses converted into two or more units. They are usually not very common and can have multiple floors, or row house-style. Their sizes could range from duplex to quad-plex (more than four units is considered commercial). Multi-family homes are different from condos as the multiple units can only be purchased together and not separately can each have separate entrances or maintain same entrance.

Pros

a. Multi-family homes are best suited for an investment property.

b. They allow families to live together but in different units.

c. Can serve both as residence for owner and rental.

d. Suitable for large families

Cons

a. Multi-Family homes can be considered a hybrid between single-family and a condo.

b. The units of multi-family are smaller in most cases than those of single family.

c. When you own a multi-family home, you bear all maintenance costs.

2. Townhouse

Townhouses are also considered a hybrid of Single-Family home and a condo. They usually have several floors with units sharing one or two walls, and would also have either a rooftop deck or a small yard space. Townhouses are usually larger than condos but small than single family.

Pros

a. Townhomes offer more privacy than can be gotten from a condo.
b. Some townhouses have agreements to share upkeep and maintenance cost.
c. They are more affordable when compared to a single family home

Cons

a. They don't usually have shared amenities.

b. They don't offer privacy as much as single family.

3. Co-op

Cooperatives, also known as co-ops are residential buildings with a shared title of ownership. This means everyone owns the building together, unlike condo where you only own your unit space. Becoming part of a co-op would often require an interview process as responsibilities are shared among owners.

Pros

a. Since they share responsibilities, cost of maintenance is low.
b. They are usually more expensive than condos

Cons

a. The shared responsibility can affect you negatively. For instance, the bank can for close on the whole building if one person stops paying their mortgage.

b. Obtaining a loan to finance a co-op could be difficult as most banks would easily finance a condo than a co-op.

4. Condominium

Also known as condos, condominiums are single units or spaces within a larger building. Condos generally share a wall or two with the other units and have homeowners associations with a monthly or yearly payment requirement. They are mostly found in high-density areas, or well-known urban areas with good economic activities.

Pros of Investing in Condos

a. **Lower purchase price.**

The purchase price of condos is usually the biggest advantage of investing in this category of residential real estate. Although prices vary from location to location, condos generally are less expensive when compared to single family homes with about 25% to 30%. Condos also have lower taxes and lower dwelling insurance cost compared to single family homes since the exterior of the building is not insured.

b. **Fewer Repairs and Maintenance to Make.** Condos incur fewer repairs to be made over time. The condo association bears the responsibility of expensive exterior repairs and maintenance. The condo investor is primarily concerned with interior enhancements.

c. **Buyer's Market.** With exception of places where real estate is very competitive, you might be pleased to know that there are fewer competitions for condos as against single-family homes.

d. **Greater Amenities for Tenants.** Condos often boost of great amenities for tenants. This is a great advantage over other form of residential homes. These include gym, swimming pool, clubhouses, etc.

Cons of investing in Condos

a. **Monthly Association Dues.**
Condos often attracts monthly association dues. It is important to know the cost of the association dues before investing as the savings gotten from lower purchase cost, taxes and insurance can easily be used to offset the due, thereby making profit less attractive.

b. **Condos are more difficult to sell.**
Another thing of note with condos is the fact that they are more difficult to sell. You will realize that by the time you wish to sell your condo, it takes more time to sell and some buyers are often reluctant to pay the full asking price for the condo.

c. **Condos are the first to drop in price in a down market.**
Between 2007 and 2010 market collapse, the value of condos depreciated faster as those

who lost their job handed back the keys to their condos back to the banks. Housing

d. **Condos are the last asset to rise in price during a recovery.**

   Condos generally have a slow recovery of value. During recovery, single family homes appreciate faster in value than condos. This is largely because the public would more readily take up offers of single-family homes first compared to condos.

e. **Unexpected assessments can affect in your profits.**

   Sometimes, condo associations would require one-time assessments to replenish reserves funds in order to cover for unexpected fixes such as foundation problems, broken pipes, repairs on amenities etc. before investing in condos, always ask if there are pending assessments to be made.

f. **Government regulations make selling a condo more difficult**.

Government regulations also affects the sale of condos. These regulations are meant to minimize the risks to mortgage holders. Some of these regulations might include restrictions on condo communities with high ratio rental units to owner occupied units by FHA lenders, restrictions on condo communities with high association dues in arrears or too many foreclosures, etc.

5. Single-Family Homes (SFH)

Single family homes (SFH) are residential homes built on a single plot, having no shared walls. The garage are sometimes detached or attached. Investments in SFH are also a great way to make passive income as one could get a good deal buying, renting out or reselling these homes depending on the time of the year.

Pros of Investing in SFH

a. Variety of Properties to Choose From

Single family homes are more readily available than any other type of residential home. There lots of option to choose in the market at any given time.

b. Find Options Below Market Value

Single family homes offer variety of possibilities to find homes that are priced below the market value. A number of factors could cause this which includes distress sell as a result of certain issues or a new agent who is unfamiliar with the market value for the area. Whatever the case is, due to the availability of single homes, one can get better deals which are below market value.

c. Smaller Upfront Investment

Single family homes offer a lower upfront payment when compared with multifamily homes. Most investors would prefer to invest smaller funds with lesser risks than investing bigger funds with higher risks in multifamily homes.

d. Financing is Simpler

It is easier to get and manage financing on single family homes. Financing is often less expensive and one can also find fixed interest rates, higher loan-to-value ratios in some cases and longer terms.

e. Zero Intra-Tenant Conflicts and Less Maintenance

One great pro of SFH is the amount of privacy that comes with it. SFH has zero conflict issues with tenants as there's only one tenant on the plot. Also maintenance needs of a single family house are much lesser and manageable than multifamily homes.

f. Better Liquidity

As a competitive commodity, single family homes are easier to sell as there are a large number of persons interested in buying. This is also an important factor to consider for a beginner who is just learning the technics in real estate. The ability to sell easily when you want is an added advantage. SFH also offer higher returns on investment upon resale. Though this varies one location to another, they generally yield good returns on investment.

Cons of Investing in Single Family Homes

a. **No Renters, No Money**

Single family homes only yield money upon resale or rental. When none of this is available, it could lead to tied up investment funds or lower ROI.

b. **Extra Fees**

Single family units most times are part of Home Owner's Association (HMO) which means there would be extra monthly fees to pay which can really add up and increase your expenses.

c. **Maintenance fee**

Investing in single family homes also means that you will bear the responsibility of maintenance of the structure. Though the cost might not be expensive when compared to multifamily homes, they however add up to your expenses and investment.

THINGS TO NOTE BEFORE INVESTING RESIDENTIAL REAL ESTATE

Residential real estate has had impressive success stories over decades with a market which continuously offers favorable broad opportunities within the sector. Investing in residential real estate however, has its own risks and challenges which should be taken into consideration prior to investments in the sector. Below are some potential risks that you might need to consider in order to have a good investment.

1. Certain Factors Affect Prices

Residential real estate remains a profitable investment with so many success stories, but there quite a number of factors that can affect prices, expenses and profit margins. Some of these include:

a. **Location:** Location is a key component to be properly taken into consideration prior to any investment. The rates and demand for any type of residential property depends on the location it is found. For instance, a single family home might will differ in price, demand and profit from one location to another. It is very important to know the value of a property within a location so as to understand how to proceed with your investment.

b. **Economic Factors:** Economic factors would also affect prices of a property. Residential properties in economically viable regions would value more than residential properties in areas with lower economic activities.

c. **Government Policies and Political Factors:** Government policies and political activities would also affect the value of residential properties. Properties located in politically unstable regions might have lower value pending the stability of the polity. Also certain government policies might increase or decrease the value of a residential property.

2. Trends Changes From Year to Year.

Trends in the property real estate are not static. This means that while a good deal is observed this year, the trend next year might change causing a depreciation in value. So it is important not to fall into the trap that trends in the sector might remain static.

3. Returns Can Be Tricky

Returns on Investment is a critical consideration for any investment. When investing in Residential properties, carefully assessing the financial viability of any property is key. It is also necessary to factor in a period of zero rentals which can affect returns projections. Properties may enjoy appreciation in capital without tenants, however, they might equally not yield any short term assistance in cash flow if nobody is paying rent.

There might also be unforeseen costs on the property and repairs which should be considered as potential risks to the cash flow.

4. Loan Values Impact Your Investments.

If you are planning on taking loans to finance your investment, it is worth considering that the same economic factors that impact your property investment and returns would also impact your loans. This means that you need to put into consideration the possibilities for interest rates to change when calculating to take out a loan to finance a property purchase. If for instance the loan is an interest variable loan, you need to factor in the risks that the loan repayments could increase above your projected returns on the property.

5. Your Capital is Tied Up

Residential real estate is considered generally as a long term investment, usually with a five-year minimum ROI. This means that returns don't come in quickly even in case that require immediate liquidation of your assets as your capital would be tied up.

INDUSTRIAL REAL ESTATE

The industrial real estate are lands and infrastructures utilized by industries or industrial businesses for mechanical production, factories, transportation, warehousing, research and development, etc. The classification of real estate as either industrial or commercial is very important because the sales, zoning and constructions are handled differently.

CATEGORIES OF INDUSTRIAL REAL ESTATE

Different types of space have different construction costs and thus have different rates of leasing and sale values. Below are the most common types of industrial real estate.

Manufacturing Industrial Space

The manufacturing category of industrial real estate deals with sites or spaces where goods are produced and assembled. They usually have loading docks for trucks, heights of at least 10 feet clear and less than 20% office space.

Properties of these characteristics vary a lot based on their purposes. The two most common types are:

a. **Heavy manufacturing:** Heavy manufacturing are giant plants with tens or hundreds of square feet usable space characterized by heavy-duty goods and materials. They usually have plenty of space for their trucks to load up products, powerful equipment usually customized to the end user and a three-phase electrical power. There is always a need for renovation and customization whenever a new owner or tenant takes up a heavy manufacturing industrial space.

b. **Light assembly:** As the name implies, the light assembly industrial spaces are a lot smaller and simpler compared with the heavy manufacturing industrial spaces. Light assembly industrial spaces are mostly used for assembling smaller parts of products,

storing and shipped from there to the
consumers. These category of industrial
spaces are easily renovated or customized by
tenants.

Storage and Distribution Industrial Space

For this category of industrial space, their sizes vary
depending on the type of property. They mostly are
comprised of about 20% office space and are mainly
used storage and logistics facility for products prior
to delivery of the products.

The three common types here are:

a. **Distribution warehouse:** These are
warehouses primarily used for shipping
goods to end users. Location is one key factor
in deciding to acquire these type of industrial
spaces. They have to be located close to easy
exit routes such as close to airports, seaports,
etc. size varies depending on the occupant.

b. **General purpose warehouses:** General
purpose warehouses are mostly aimed at

handling storage more than distribution. For general purpose warehouses, locations are not a key determinant, rather size is considered more, as this impacts what is to be stored.

c. **Truck terminal:** The truck terminal is the third type of storage and distribution industrial space. They mostly are intermediate sites used for transferring or loading goods from one truck to another.

Flex Space

Flex industrial spaces are generally spaces that offer the tenants the flexibility of customizing to fit their usage. They generally have at least up to 30% office space, a ground-level or dock-head doors at the back, offices with glass front entries, and car park. Some flex space are more customized for special clients. These include:

a. **R&D:** These are flex spaces customized for Research and Development (R&D) purposes. These type of spaces vary depending on the tenant and what they will be using the space for.

b. **Data Center:** These kinds of flex spaces are to keep data equipment, ensure internet is running effectively and also make cloud storage possible. The average size is about 100,000 square feet but could also get bigger. For example, the world's largest data center is found in Lanfang, China with 6.3 million square foot. Data centers are quite competitive and have high market demand. Example, car dealerships.

c. **Showrooms:** showrooms are a combination of offices, warehousing and showrooms. Although more than half of the space is usually allotted for showcasing and selling products.

BENEFITS OF INVESTING IN INDUSTRIAL RETAIL ESTATE

Industrial real estate offers some good ROI among other benefits. Some of the major benefits include:

a. Higher Rents = Higher Yields

With the large spaces involved, industrial real estate also attracts higher rents with ultimately yields higher returns. Industrial spaces are generally valued in relation to their square meters and can offer ROI projections of about 8% which is quite an interesting offer when compared to 4% - 5% on some residential real estate. Another aspect of returns for industrial spaces is the fixed annual price increases for most industrial spaces which often times are linked to CPI.

b. Longer Leases

In industrial real estate, tenants usually agree to sign longer lease agreements, up to 10 years in most case. This provides the investor with greater guarantee and security compared to residential properties.

c. Net Leases

Industrial real estate offer the advantage of net lease for most spaces. This simply means that the tenant would pay for costs that the owner of the property or investor would normally have paid. These include utilities, insurance, repair, and maintenance costs.

d. Low-Maintenance Buildings

For industries who take up industrial spaces, they would brand and maintain these properties to reflect their brands. This means that there will be low maintenance needs as the tenants would normally handle any maintenance needs urgently.

RISK FACTORS TO CONSIDER IN INDUSTRIAL REAL ESTATE

As stated earlier, every investment carries a potential risk which must be taken into consideration before investing. Thus, it is very important to understand the potential risks in industrial real estate investment. Below are a few of the key risks you need to consider:

a. Vacancy risks

Industrial properties tend to have higher risks of vacancy as they are more susceptible to market conditions. When a business closes or moves out of a property, it could take a longer time for a new client to move in. This means that investors in industrial real estate should be prepared to have longer waits or long periods of vacancy.

b. Expensive to invest

Industrial properties requires huge financing and as a result, are seen as riskier investments by banks and this makes the cost of borrowing higher. Banks also demand larger deposit of around 30% with interest rates higher than those of the residential property.

c. Obsolescence

As a constantly evolving and innovating sector, industrial buildings can become obsolete over short period of time due to reasons such as, clearance height becoming too low, limited access to the property or the floor space not being suitable for modern machines. Location can equally become a reason for obsolescence.

COMMERCIAL REAL ESTATE

Commercial real estate are properties or infrastructures intended or used by businesses for their businesses operations. These include individual stores, shopping centers, office buildings, medical centers, educational buildings etc.

CATEGORIES OF COMMERCIAL REAL ESTATE.

Discussed below are the 5 common types of commercial real estate properties.

a. Office Buildings

This category of buildings can be multi-tenanted, single, or build-to-suit lease and can be further classified into suburban and urban properties. While the suburban buildings (also called mid-rise structures) are found outside of the city, the urban buildings (also known as high-rise properties) can be located downtown area of the city. There are 3 classes of office buildings:

- Class A: These class of structures are considered the most prestigious buildings in commercial real estate. They usually have the best amenities, technology and are located in prime locations.
- Class B: Class B buildings are the class of office buildings that are a little older, but still retain good quality and management. They can be found in a mix of location but can't be categorized as Class A
- Class C: These are found in less desirable locations, are a lot older and would require a lot of renovation. They are thus the lowest classification of office buildings.

b. **Industrial Properties**

Industrial properties as a type of real estate investment can be classified as a type of commercial real estate because they are generally used by businesses for different purpose. Industrial properties have been discussed previously as a type of real estate but they generally include manufacturing facilities, storage and distribution spaces, and flex spaces.

c. Retail Centers

These are a type of office spaces used by restaurants, grocery stores, strip malls, regional outlet malls and shopping centers among others. These type of space can be multi-tenanted, single or stand-alone-buildings.

d. Multifamily Complex

A multifamily complex is any structure that has more than four separate apartments. This would include downtown high-rise apartments, condos, and apartment complexes. Multifamily complexes are usually classified from A to D.

- Class A: This class comprises of the luxury apartment found in prime locations with top amenities such as swimming pool, gym, cafes, etc.
- Class B: This class comprises of structures that usually are 10-25 years old. They are well maintained and their rental fees are a bit lower than those of class A.
- Class C: In this class are the buildings that are more than 20 year old. They are usually found in prime locations but require renovations and repairs and usually have lower rental rates than class A and B.
- Class D: Here the buildings are more than 30 years old and might have worn due to high turnover. Their locations are in less desirable areas.

e. Commercial Land

This is the last category of commercial real estate and includes vacant or undeveloped land intended for business use. Examples includes parking lots, warehouses, or any income generating venture. The location of commercial land large determines the varying value of the land.

BENEFITS OF COMMERCIAL REAL ESTATE INVESTMENT

a. Income Potential.

The earning potential from commercial real estate investment remains one of the top benefits of investing in commercial properties. They usually offer up to 6%-12% annual ROI projections as against those of single family homes of around 4%.

b. More Objective Price Evaluations.

Commercial properties are more easily evaluated because an investor can request for the current owners income statement to determine what the price should be based on the statement. In a case where a broker is used by the seller, the asking price is set at a price where an investor earns the prevailing cap rate for the property type. Commercial properties generally receive more objective pricing evaluation compared to residential which tend to receive more emotional pricing.

c. Triple Net Leases.

The concept of triple net leases is that the investor or owner of the property does not have to pay any expenses on the property in order to maintain the look and feel of their brands. The tenants handles all property expenses, including taxes. The only expense handled by the investor/owner is the mortgage. Net leases and triple net leases come are not for smaller businesses or residential properties.

d. Professional relationships.

Commercial properties could serve as a channel of building business relationships. Commercial properties are usually not owned by individuals but LLCs and as such would improve interactions and business relationship of both parties.

e. More flexibility in lease terms.

Unlike the many state laws, termination rules, and security deposit limits that govern residential properties, fewer consumer protection laws govern commercial properties.

RISK FACTORS TO CONSIDER IN COMMERCIAL REAL ESTATE.

Investing in commercial real estate like every other real estate category offers great rewards and great risks alike. To maximize opportunities and profit, an you should understand the the potential risks, pit falls and prepare to avoiding.

a. Huge Capital and Financing:

One of the major risks to consider in commercial properties, is the huge financing and capital involved. These properties varies and are handled by professionals who would keep things as professional as possible. Without the required capital or financing, it is almost impossible to invest in commercial properties.

b. Economic Downturn

Another risk factor to consider in commercial real estate is the potential impact of the economy on your investment. If for instance, there occurs an economic downturn, which affects businesses causing them to either shut down operations, it simply means your investment will produce little or no income for that period. This in turn will affect your cash flow and your ROI projections. However, with reserve capital, you can cushion the effect of economic downturn on your investment.

c. Adequate Industry Knowledge

Commercial real estate investment requires and in-depth industry knowledge for proper analysis of properties to avoid loss of investment. It is always better to work with professionals who know the ropes and can properly guide against pitfalls.

d. It Ties Up Your Capital

As an investment with huge capital and long term projections, commercial properties might take a while to be sold or leased and you have to have the ability to bear expenses on the property.

REAL ESTATE DEMOGRAPHICS

Demographics are data which gives the comprehensive composition of a population. This includes race, age, income, gender, population growth and migration patterns. In real estate investments, these statistics are very vital indicators that affect pricing and property demand but are often overlooked by investors. Shifts in demographics would always have huge impact on real estate trends and investment projections.

Demographics helps investors narrow down on location and type of real estate investments to venture in. Other importance of real estate demographics include:

a. Demographics help review and analyze locations of proposed investment property
b. They give an overview of asset performance
c. Helps you understand other factors that can affect your investment's performance and profit projections.

DEMOGRAPHICS THAT AFFECTS REAL ESTATE INVESTMENTS

An in-depth analysis of the demographics of the location of your real estate investment will provide you with useful insights regarding your prospective investment. Below are some real estate demographics that could affect your real estate investment.

a. Population Growth

One key demographic factor that can affect real estate is the population growth rate of the location and population growth depends on factors such as affordable living cost, access to variety of industries, entrepreneurship and low unemployment rate. The migration of people to an area implies a rising number of potential tenants and buyers. As an investor, identifying areas with rising population and a rising housing demand, increases the potentials of your property appreciating in price as these growths would translate into rental shortages and rising rents. Thus this assures of better cash flow and higher profits, especially for buy and hold investments.

b. Amenities

Amenities such as roads, quality school, utilities, educated neighbors, ocean view and beautiful architecture are factors that can affect your real estate investment. For example, most families try to balance Median Home Value with quality school ratings. This means investing in neighborhoods with school quality rankings can positively influence demands for your property, pricing and profits.

c. Crime Risk/Security

Crime risk and security are important factors to consider prior to investing in any property as people generally want to feel safe and secure within their environment. In his studies, Dr. Steve Gibbons of the LSE discovered that a 10% reduction in recorded crime adds around 1.7% to the selling price of an average home within a neighborhood. Local crime rates if ignored by the investor has the potential to impact the values of the real estate, insurance rates and the investments.

d. High-Paying Jobs And Opportunities

One of the biggest factors in deciding on an investment location is the rate of Job growth and employment opportunities within the location. If there are no Jobs or opportunities to find jobs, people will not be interested in migrating to that location. This also means lower interest in rentals or purchase of properties within the location. As an investor it is necessary to observe the income and employment opportunities and trends.

e. Ratio Of Tenants Vs. Owners

The ratio of rentals vs. Owner-occupied homes is another very important key factor to consider. Depending on what you are looking for, either of this could be bad or good for a certain region or neighborhood. If for instance you you're out for income properties, rental-oriented areas would be the best for your investment. However, if you're looking out for fix and flip investments, the same rental-oriented areas will make it difficult to sell. Always pay detailed attention to the average rates of rentals, and sales price within your investment location.

f. The Community/Neighborhood

The community where your investment or proposed investment is located is another important demographic factor for consideration. For a community with a large number of young families, investing in multifamily apartments will give better ROI. Also if investing in commercial properties is your interest, an area full of business would be an optimal choice for investing. Ensure to always have a general look on the community of your proposed investment. Take into account things, networking opportunities, child-friendly activities, local businesses etc.

REAL ESTATE INVESTMENT INCOME AND TYPES

There are basically two investment principles or income path in the investment world, including real estate investment. These two paths are distinct from each other and represent a desired investment interest. They are:

1. Capital gain investment

2. Cash flow investment

The best way to successfully invest in real estate is first to be clear on the investment path to follow, which also will be determined by the investment interest or desired outcome. Following an investment income path will help you measure your investment successes of failures. It also should be noted that no investment path is superior to the other. The bottom line lies on your interest and desired outcome.

1. Real Estate Capital Gain Investment

Capital gain investment path in real estate is the art of buying properties or assets at relatively below market value and selling them for profit when it appreciates in value. In capital gain investment, an investor researches and identifies an undervalued property, purchases and improves the property and sells it at a much higher price (at maturity stage) after a period of time. Thus, capital gains investment relies typically on the fundamentals purchasing undervalued real estate assets and selling after the value appreciates over a period of time.

For example, an investors purchases a single family home with an investment capital of $100,000 and over the course of 10 months he puts in and extra $20,000 in renovations and maintenance making a total investment of $120,000. if after two months or thereabout the investor sells the property for $180,000, he makes a profit of $60,000 (50% profit on investment) in one year after deducting his initial investment capital and any additional investment made. This type of investment is called capital gains investment. As can be seen, the investor purchased the property at a lower market value, improves the property over a period of time, thus improving the value and selling at a higher price.

Capital gains investments are classified into two:

    a. Short Term Investments: These are investments whose terms are not more than one year.

    b. Long Term Investments: These are investments whose terms are above one year.

RISK FACTORS TO CONSIDER IN REAL ESTATE CAPITAL GAINS INVESTMENT

    a. **Not a Continuous Income Flow:** Capital gains investment capital does not guarantee a steady flow of income. Income is primarily dependent of sales of property at any given time. This simply means that you have to keep buying and selling properties to make income.

    b. **Market Crisis:** Capital investment can be easily hit by market crisis at any given time. If the market takes a nosedive at any point, it will be difficult to get buyers for your property. This will equally affect your investment profit projection and profits as the case may be.

c. **Capital Loss**: While there are success stories on capital investment, there are also potentials of having capital loss. Capital loss occurs when an asset or real estate investment is sold below purchase or invested capital value. A number of factors can lead to this such as market crisis, demographics, etc.

If you have chosen capital gains as your investment path, ensure to always do thorough research on any asset before investing. Other best practices to note in capital gains investments are:

a. Don't speculate
b. Don't sell because the market is in crisis
c. Be patient with your investment
d. Sell when the property no longer holds the initial value for which you bought it. This means the property must have appreciated

e. Understand that there might be losses, so follow due diligence.

2. Real Estate Cash Flow

Real estate cash flow simply refers to the art of purchasing an investment and holding on to it with the expectations of receiving a monthly, quarterly or yearly returns constantly from it through rents. Regardless of the time frame involved, the fundamental principle of cash flow is the constant flow of income from your investment and building wealth.

Unlike the capital gains investors, cash flow inventors are not concerned with selling their investments at higher market value, rather, they keep their investments and collect regular income from it. The cash flow model helps keep your eyes of short term market movements and helps you build wealth with the constant flow of income.

For instance, if you purchase a multifamily house, fix it up and rent it out rather than sell it, you have adopted the cash flow model. Every month, quarter or year, you collect rent while also bearing the responsibility of paying expenses such as mortgage for the investment.

CASH FLOW ANALYSIS – HOW TO DETERMINE CASH FLOW

Calculating cash flow on rental property is relatively simple if you have the right data available to you. While this is simple to calculate, it is necessary to carry out due diligence as there are a number of things to account for in order to get a fairly accurate analysis. Also bear in mind that cash flow analysis can only give you an estimate and not actual figures as there are so many other factors that may never be envisaged which might influence the actual figure. Below are more detailed ways of calculating rental cash flow projections for your investment.

1. Standard Method

The standard method is the simplest way to calculate cash flow on rental properties. To use the standard method,

a. **Add all Income**: calculating rental cash flow begins with identifying how much income you are expecting over the course of one year from rents. The best way to find out how much you can get from rents from your property is to accurately compare local properties similar to yours within the neighborhood. This might also involve speaking to local realtors or property management firms in order to get accurate values of what your property would rent for. Having got the monthly accurate figure, multiply by 12 to give an annual income.

b. **Subtract All Expenses:** Having calculated your income, the next step is to subtract all expense you expect to make on your property. This should include mortgage payment, taxes, labor and maintenance and every expenses related to the property.

Cash Flow (Standard Method) = Total Income – Total Expenditure

The result of this calculation will give you the estimated cash flow from your rental property. As earlier stated, ensure to get an accurate date in order to get a fairly accurate estimation.

2. Annual Cash Flow Investment Properties

The standard method is more useful in estimating cash flow during a short period of time and not over a longer time span. The standard method also does not take into account the return rate of the total investment. There are two annual cash flow method here.

a. **Cash on Cash Return:** This method which is expressed in percentage, is used to calculate the long-term performance of a real estate investment. It simply is the property's net annual cash flow divided by the net investment.

Cash on Cash Return = (Annual Cash Flow/Total Cash Invested) × 100%

An 8% or higher yield from cash on cash return is considered a good investment.

b. The 50% Rule: The 50% rule does not have much practical application. It is more useful in quickly comparing multiple rental properties for a manual market analysis. Besides this, it is limited in use. The standard and cash on cash methods are more practical.

Cash Flow (50% Rule) = (Total Income × 50%) – Mortgage Principal and Interest.

Other Real Estate Cash Flow Analysis Tools

a. Models, Charts, and Projections

Models, charts and projections are three of the most common cash flow analysis tools among several others. They serve majorly the same purpose which is to estimate future cash flow analysis but are slightly different in data presentation. The chart visualizes information, the models and projections present information in a spreadsheet format.

b. Investment Property Calculator

An investment property calculator works as an interactive and very efficient tool for cash flow forecast. While the models, charts and projections are used manually, the investment property calculator tends to be faster and easier to use. The investor will only have to insert variables and the calculator will present the investment forecast within a short time.

Why Real Estate Cash Flow Analysis Is Important

    a. Informs you about profits or losses

    b. It identifies potential flaws in any investment

    c. It helps you compares between potential properties, and make informed decisions.

WHY INVEST IN REAL ESTATE?

While real estate investment is not always glamorous, it still remains one of the best and sure ways to build wealth over a long period of time. Below are some reasons why real estate investment in not just good but outstanding and why you should get in as soon as possible.

1. Cash flow

As explained in our previous section, cash flow income is one of the best reasons to invest in real estate. Real estate cash flow can provide you with stable passive income and give you enough time to focus on other activities you choose to engage in.

2. Tax Benefits

Real estate investments enjoys varied tax benefits. Cash flow from real estate investments are not subject to self-employment tax and the government gives tax benefits such as depreciation and very low tax-rates from long-term profits.

3. The Loan Pay Down

If real estate investment is purchased using mortgage, your tenant actually pays the mortgage, thus increasing your net worth each month. As a result of loan pay down, a rental property could serve as a savings account without you paying deposit every month.

4. Appreciation

Real estate despite the times of market crisis is known to appreciate in value over long period of time.

5. Ah Hedge Against Inflation

Inflation is the continuous rise of prices as a result of the decreasing value of money. Real estate serves a hedge where by as inflation increases, the value of properties also increase thus increasing cash flow.

6. Control

In real estate, the investor has control over his investment and financial future. He could decide to flip, buy and hold, buy, develop and rent, etc. He has control over his investment.

REAL ESTATE INVESTMENT FINANCING – Ways To Finance Your First Real Estate Investment.

Financing your first real estate investment might look like a herculean task at first, but having a proper information on the several ways to finance your investment especially as a beginner, will go a long way in getting you off the ground easily with your first investment.

In the real estate sector, most investors often pick up properties without putting their own money down. They finance the whole investment and still make healthy profits.

Below are some ways you can access to fund your first acquisition.

a. Use FHA Loan (If in USA)
FHA stands for Federal Housing Administration. For your first acquisition, you can obtain a mortgage insured by FHA with a little as 3.5% down payment.

With this you can acquire a multifamily house, occupy one part and rent the other part.

b. Hard Money Loans

Another great option is to obtain hard money loans. Though these loans tend to have higher interest rates and are not sustainable for long term, they give you the flexibility to close quick deals. Good deals actually don't last long as they are very competitive, thus hard money loans can get you started until you acquire traditional loans.

c. Non-Bank Mortgage Lending

There are quite a number of non-bank lenders who are willing to offer financing for your investment. This is coming against the backdrop of how difficult it is becoming to qualify for mortgages in traditional banks. These lenders are quick in closing deals compared to banks and sometimes can offer up to 100% of the acquisition.

d. Funding From Family and Friends

Funding through family and friends require not capital. You could reach out to a number of family and friends and have them pull funds together to close a deal. If funds are minimal, you can use the minimal funds and go through FHA as mentioned earlier.

e. Trust Deed Investing

Trust deed investing involves taking mortgage from either a family member, friend or any private lender who will function as the bank. You will give to them a deed of trust to serve as collateral on the property, thereby agreeing to lending terms. If for any reason you don't meet up the terms, the private lender just like the bank will move in and foreclose on the property.

BEST WAYS TO MAKE MONEY FROM REAL ESTATE

Real estate investment is one of the ways to build wealth as there are quite a number of ways to make money from this thriving sector. We shall look at some of the channels through which income can be generated from real estate, however, you'd need to carry out an in-depth analysis such as estimating valuations, estimating ROI, and financing options available, in order to determine which strategy to follow.

1. Buy-and-Hold Real Estate Investing

Buy-and-hold real estate investing is one of the most popular real estate channels for income generation. Buy-and-hold involves the acquisition of a rental property with the aim of holding it for a long period of time. In Buy-and-Hold real estate investment, income generation is through monthly, quarterly or yearly rents paid to the investor while the value of the investment appreciates over the years. Buy-and-hold guarantees the investor a constant cash flow from the investment.

Buy-and-hold can be a good way for any beginner to start making money from real estate while building wealth over time. It is relatively easy to begin and doesn't require much experience. Alternatively, you can hire a professional to manage your properties.

There are different types of buy-and-hold investments to choose from. These include:

a. **Vacation Rental Property**: This investment strategy involves renting out vacation properties, thereby offsetting some costs of home ownership.

b. **Multifamily Property:** Here, the strategy is to acquire a property with 2-4 units and then renting either part or all of it.

c. **Commercial Real Estate:** In commercial real estate, the focus is on acquiring properties that can be rented out for business purposes.

d. **Turnkey Real Estate:** In turnkey investment, the property is usually a move-in-ready apartment which comes with tenants and property Management Company in place.

e. Apartment Building: This is an investment in property with 5 and more units, generating incomes from rents, vending and parking revenue.

Benefits of Buy-and-Hold Real Estate Investing

a. Monthly cash flow income
b. Tax reduction benefits
c. Build equity as tenants pay down your mortgage
d. Appreciation in property value

2. Real Estate Trading: Property Flipping

In real estate trading also known as flipping, investors buy properties with the purpose of selling them after holding for a short period, usually not more than four months. This is another great strategy to make money from real estate. The fundamental rule of flipping is that the investor looks out for properties that are either undervalued or are in a competitive location, acquires them and resells after a very short period at a higher value.

There are two categories of property flippers.

    a. The first category of flippers who purchase properties and do not make any improvements on the property. They believe the investment has the potential value to make profit without renovation. These investments are usually short-term.

    b. The second category of flippers are the investors who buy properties at below market value, improves on them and sells them at a higher price. Depending on the extent of renovations, this can be long term investments.

3. Real Estate Investment Groups

Real estate investment groups are another way to make income from real estate, especially if you do not intend to go through the stress of managing the property. Here, a company buys or develops a set of buildings or apartment and opens up these apartments for purchase to investors through them (the company), thus forming a group. An investor can own one or more of these apartments but the company operating the investment group manages all units for all investors and collects a percentage of the rent.

4. Real Estate Limited Partnerships (RELP)

Real Estate Limited Partnership is quite similar to real estate investment groups only that it is formed in other to acquire and hold single or multiple properties for a given number of years. A property manager or real estate development company would serve as the general partner and invite investors to finance the project(s) in exchange of ownerships as limited partners. Investors would receive incomes periodically and a pay off when the properties are sold. This is another way of making income from real estate investment. Similar to real estate group investments, it saves you the stress of managing, and maintaining the properties.

5. Real Estate Investment Trust (REIT)

A real estate investment trust is formed by a trust or corporation in order to use the finance of investors to purchase, operate and sell income yielding properties. Like stocks, real estate investment trusts are bought and sold on major exchanges and to avoid paying corporate income tax, REITs pay out dividends which are 90% of its taxable profits.

To make income from REIT, you would need to purchase REITs from exchanges and profit from dividends that are shared among investors. This is another way of making money from real estate without actually owning a property.

MAKING MONEY THROUGH REAL ESTATE AGENCY

Real estate over the years has turned out to be a lucrative and rewarding business and as also created many streams of income generation and wealth creation. It has also created several value chains with diverse opportunities for success. As a beginner, besides being an investor, there are other ways of generating income from the real estate industry without actually owning or investing in any real estate portfolio. One of such ways it through real estate agency.

A real estate agency (a corporation or company) or agent (individual) is a professional who executes real estate transactions, bringing together sellers and buyers, acting as their representatives during negotiations and earning income form commissions which usually is a percentage of the price for which the property was sold.

As a sector with huge opportunities, the real estate market size can be estimated from the statistics of the

U.S market. In 2017, 5.51 million housing units were sold with the figure expected to rise up to 5.67 million by the end of 2019. Statistics also showed commercial properties sold were about 74.24 billion U.S. dollars. This clearly shows how lucrative the real estate market is and the huge potentials it has both for investors and agents. Below we shall discuss some of the ways to make money through real estate agency.

1. Become a Buyer's Agent.

A buyer agent primarily works as the representative of investors looking to buy properties. The agent takes the buyer to different location to access the properties, write offers on houses and handle the entire process of purchase for the buyer. As a buyer's agent, you make money through commissions and based on the number of buyers you have.

2. List Homes for Sellers

Here, the agent is known as a listing agent or agency and works with the sellers unlike the buyer's agent. The duty of a listing agent includes helping sellers find the right price for the property they want sold, prepare it for sale and listing the property or properties for sale. The listing agent negotiates with buyers, handles all sales transactions and collects commissions (a given percentage of the purchase price).

3. Sell short Sales.

A short sale is when a listing agent negotiates with a bank to accept a lesser amount from a home owner who is not able to sell of their property at a price that can cover their loan repayment. If the bank accepts the amount, the agent then list's the seller's home at a normal price. The agent will also handle all legal processes with a short sale. The drawback to this is that negotiations with the bank can take up to months before it accepts the amount.

4. Prepare Broker Price Opinions (BPO)

Broker Price Opinion is a report by licensed appraisers to value homes. A BPO compares several homes with relevant statistics for optimal pricing and for the benefit of the seller. Preparing BPO can earn an agent around $30 to $100 but the agent must be licensed. Preparing BPO is relatively easy and requires a physical inspection of the homes or analyzing the exterior pictures of the homes.

5. Become a Property Manager

Property management is another way of making money through agency. As a property manager, your duties incudes maintaining, managing, fixing damages, renting (finding renters and collecting rents), and generally overseeing your client's property. Property managers collect a certain percentage of the rent they manage (up to 10%), and earn money from leasing fees.

6. Become a Commercial Real Estate Agent

Commercial real estate agents are paid on a monthly basis and this is because they have a vast and extensive knowledge of valuing commercial properties. They are paid more than residential agents who only earn on commission basis.

7. Become a Broker

A real estate broker is one who manages a group of real estate agents under his firm. As a broker you ensure that all agents under you follow and abide by legal processes in any transaction. In a case of legal dispute, a broker handles all legal matters.

As a broker, you get a percentage of the commissions from the agents you manage, desk fees and adverts.

CONCLUSION

As can be seen, the real estate industry, though with its ups and downs like every other business, is a highly lucrative sector with lots of opportunities even for beginners. To be successful, largely depends on your ability to first figure out where you want to start from and be detailed in your analysis.

Whatever niche you choose within the numerous value chain in real estate, you can be sure of success and wealth creation.

www.ingramcontent.com/pod-product-compliance
Lightning Source LLC
Chambersburg PA
CBHW070919220526
45467CB00004B/1473